# LAWS

OF THE

# CHEROKEE NATION,

PASSED AT

TAHLEQUAH, CHEROKEE NATION,

**1844-5.**

---

# LAWS

OF

# THE CHEROKEE NATION.

PASSED AT THE ANNUAL SESSION

OF THE

**NATIONAL COUNCIL,**

**1845.**

---

SR Scholarly Resources Inc.
1508 Pennsylvania Avenue · Wilmington, Delaware 19806

SCHOLARLY RESOURCES, INC.
Wilmington, Delaware • London

Reprint edition published in 1975

Library of Congress Catalog Card Number: 75-3668
ISBN: 0-8420-1835-2

Manufactured in the United States of America

# LAWS

OF THE

# CHEROKEE NATION,

PASSED AT

TAHLEQUAH, CHEROKEE NATION,

**1844-5.**

---

TAHLEQUAH,

**Printed at the office of the Cherokee Advocate.**

1845.

# LAWS
## OF
# THE CHEROKEE NATION,
## PASSED AT THE ANNUAL SESSION OF THE NATIONAL COUNCIL, 1844–5.

---

*Resolved by the National Council*, That the Principal Chief be, and he is hereby authorized, to have five hundred copies of the laws of the Cherokee Nation, enacted during the present session of the council, printed in both the Cherokee and English languages.

*And be it further resolved*, That he is hereby requested, to have the same completed by the close of the present session of the Council, if practicable.

*And be it further resolved*, That the Principal Chief be, and he is hereby, authorized to have the same distributed throughout the several districts, as soon as completed.

TAHLEQUAH, C. N., Jan. 6th, 1845.

MOSES DANIEL,
*Pres't Nat. Com.*

Concurred: A. CAMPBELL,
*Speaker Council pro tem.*

---

AN ACT to re-organize Police companies.

*Be it enacted by the National Council*, That there be, forthwith organized, eight Police companies, one to each district; to be composed of twenty-five armed men each, whose duty shall be to suppress all conspiracies, and to apprehend and bring to justice, all persons charged with treason against the Government of this Nation.

*Be it further enacted*, That each company aforesaid, shall be under the command of one Captain and one Lieutenant, who shall be elected by joint vote of the National Council. Each Captain shall raise his own company.—In case of the death, resignation, or inability of any Captain, the Lieutenant of such company shall assume the command.

*Be it further enacted*, That the said companies and officers shall be under the command of a Colonel, to be elected in the manner above prescribed, who shall inspect the companies, instruct them in their duties and in the exercise of vigilance, in ferreting out and bringing such persons to justice. Whenever occasion requires, he shall concentrate as many of the companies at any place, as he may deem necessary for sustaining the laws and interests of the Nation. He shall be subject to the orders and instructions of the Executive, advise with him, and regularly report to him whatever information he may possess, relative to the movement of the companies.

*Be it further enacted*, That the Colonel shall receive three dollars, each Captain two dollars, each Lieutenant one dollar and fifty cents, and each private one dollar per day, while engaged in actual service. The term of service of said companies shall be one year.

*Be it further enacted*, That the Captains aforesaid, shall make monthly returns to the Colonel, of the expenses of their respective companies, for horse-shoeing and ferriages; powder, lead and flints; provisions and forage, (to be bought at the cheapest rates;) and said returns, to be transmitted regularly by the Colonel, to the Principal Chief.

*Be it further enacted*, That all the officers aforesaid, shall be commissioned according to rank, by the Principal Chief, and bound by oath to support the Constitution and Laws of the Cherokee Nation.

TAHLEQUAH, C. N., *Oct. 18th*, 1844.

THOMAS FOREMAN,
*Pres't. Nat. Committee pro tem.*
RICHARD DREW,
*Speaker pro tem of the Council.*
WILL. P. ROSS,
*Clerk Nat. Committee.*
J. MULKEY,
*Clerk Council.*

Approved: MOSES DANIEL,
*Acting Principal Chief.*

---

AN ACT relating to a Commissary.

*Be it enacted by the National Council*, That there shall be elected, annually, by a joint vote of the National Council, one issuing Commissary.

*Be it further enacted*, That it shall be the duty of the said Commissary, to attend at the opening of the annual, or any legally called Council, for the purpose of receiving, and receipting for all corn, beef and salt, of good wholesome quality, that may be tendered by contractors, and issuing the same to the public Cooks, according to an economical calculation, made by him of daily consumption. He shall see that the public Cooks are faithful in the discharge of their duties; and furnish to each Council, true returns of the quantity of provisions received by him, from contractors.

*Be it further enacted*, That the said Commissary shall be allowed, out of the National Treasury, a compensation of one dollar and fifty cents per day, while in actual service. Before entering upon his duties, he shall be required to execute to the National Treasurer, a bond, with approved security, in the penal sum of five hundred dollars, for their faithful discharge.

*Be it further enacted*, That the first election under this Act, shall take place before the final adjournment of the present National Council, and the person then elected as Commissary, shall enter upon his duties, at the opening of the annual Council in 1845, or at any Council that may be called previous to that time, by the proper authorities of the Nation.

TAHLEQUAH, C. N., *Oct.* 21*st*, 1844.

THOMAS FOREMAN,
*Pres't Nat. Com. pro tem.*
RICHARD DREW,
*Speaker pro tem of the Council.*
Approved: MOSES DANIEL,
*Acting Principal Chief.*

---

*Be it enacted by the National Council*, That the Principal Chief be, and he is hereby authorized to appoint, for the term of one year, a third printer, to be engaged in the office of the Cherokee Advocate, in addition to the two printers, provided for in the Act, passed, October 25th, 1843, establishing a National Printing Press, &c.

*Be it further enacted*, That the printer so appointed, shall be subject to the requirements of the aforesaid Act, and shall receive, for his services, three hundred dollars per annum.

TAHLEQUAH, C. N., *Oct.* 24*th*, 1844.

THOMAS FOREMAN,
*Pres't Nat. Com. pro tem.*
Concurred: JAMES M. PAYNE,
*Speaker Council.*
Approved: MOSES DANIEL,
*Acting Principal Chief.*

---

**AN ACT** to repeal an Act, entitled an "Act to amend an Act, passed Sep. 23d, 1839, establishing the Judiciary."

*Be it enacted by the National Council*, That an Act, passed Oct. 15th, 1841, entitled "an Act, to amend an

Act passed Sept. 23d, 1839, establishing the Judiciary," be, and the same is hereby repealed.

TAHLEQUAH, C. N., Oct. 29th, 1844.

JAMES M. PAYNE,
*Speaker Council.*

THOMAS FOREMAN,
*Pres't Nat. Com. pro tem.*

Approved: JNO. JOSS.

---

AN ACT prohibiting betting on elections.

*Be it enacted by the National Council*, That hereafter, all betting on elections, held in this Nation, is declared to be unlawful, and any person or persons who shall be found guilty of violating the provision of this Act, before any legally constituted Court, shall, for each and every such offence, be fined, at the discretion of the Court, in a sum, not less than fifty, nor more than five hundred dollars; one half of such fine shall be for the benefit of the informer, and the other half be paid into the National Treasury.

TAHLEQUAH, C. N., Nov. 1st, 1844.

THOMAS FOREMAN,
*Pres't Nat. Com. pro tem.*

Concurred: RICHARD DREW,
*Speaker pro tem Council.*

Approved: JNO. ROSS.

---

AN ACT for determining elections in case of tie.

*Be it enacted by the National Council*, That hereafter, in any election, for members of the National Committee, or Council, or Sheriffs, when two or more candidates shall receive an equal number of votes, the Principal Chief, upon receiving notification of the fact from the Superintendants of such election, shall immediately issue a writ authorizing the holding of another election in the district in which such tie may occur.

TAHLEQUAH, C. N., Nov. 1st, 1844.

THOMAS FOREMAN,
*Pres't Nat. Com. pro tem.*

Concurred: RICHARD DREW,
*Speaker pro tem Council.*

Approved: JNO. ROSS.

---

AN ACT to regulate Grist Mills.

*Be it enacted by the National Council*, That, from and after the 1st of January next, the owners of grist mills, established in the Cherokee Nation, shall be held accountable, and made pay for any bag and grain, which may be lost, left in their charge in the mill; provided, however, that the bags are marked or branded by the owners.

TAHLEQUH, C. NATION, Nov. 6th, 1844.

JAMES M. PAYNE,
*Speaker Council.*

Concurred: MOSES DANIEL,
*Pres't Nat. Com.*

Approved: JNO. ROSS.

---

AN ACT to amend an Act establishing the Judiciary.

*Be it enacted by the National Council*, That an Act, passed 23d September, 1839, entitled "an Act establishing the Judiciary," be, and the same is hereby so amended, that if any of the Circuit or District Judges shall be interested, by consanguinity, or otherwise, in the termination of any suit that may be pending in their respective Courts, and either of the parties to such suit shall object to his presiding in its trial, he shall transmit such objections to the Principal Chief, who shall appoint another Judge to preside until such suit is decided, provided that such objections are made at the time the suit is instituted, and are accompanied with good and sufficient reasons.—Any person who may be appointed special Judge under the foregoing enactment, shall be allowed three dollars per day, out of the National Treasury, while in actual service.

*Be it further enacted*, That the above named Act, be, and the same is hereby further amended, so that if any person constituting in part, a jury for the trial of civil cases, shall be interested in the termination of any suit that may require his decision, the Judge of the Court, shall have the right, on the application of either of the parties, setting forth by oath, satisfactory evidence of such fact, to appoint a new jury entire, or in part, for the trial of such case.

TAHLEQUAH, C. N., *Nov 9th*, 1844.

MOSES DANIEL,
*Pres't Nat. Com.*

Concurred: JAMES M. PAYNE,
*Speaker Council.*

---

AN ACT for the benefit of G. W. Corbin, Contractor.

*Be it enacted by the National Council*, That the sum of nine hundred and seventy-two dollars, be, and the same is hereby appropriated, out of any moneys in the National Treasury, not otherwise appropriated, for the benefit and use of Geo. W. Corbin, Contractor for building a Printing office, at Tahlequah, of the kind and description, set forth in an Act passed at the last session of the annual Council, authorizing the building of a Printing office.

*Be it further enacted*, That the Principal Chief be, and he is hereby authorized to draw a warrant on the National Treasury, for the amount of the above appropriation, in the name of the said Geo. W. Corbin, Contractor.

TAHLEQUAH, *Nov. 11th*, 1844.

MOSES DANIEL,
*Pres't N. Committee.*

Concurred, JAMES M. PAYNE,
*Speaker Council.*

Approved: JNO. ROSS.

---

AN ACT to amend an Act, for the punishment of criminal offences.

*Be it enacted by the National Council*, That an Act, passed the 9th of September, 1839, for the punishment of criminal offences, be, and the same is hereby amended, in the first section, to read as follows: "And when sentence of death shall have been passed, the Court shall grant a respite of five days, before such criminal be executed," and in all cases, where a criminal, under sentence of death, shall escape before the day of execution, and afterwards be apprehended, he shall be delivered to the Sheriff of the district, where the trial was had, and after two days from the time of his delivery, the Sheriff shall proceed to execute the sentence of death.

TAHLEQUAH, C. N., Nov. 11th, 1844.

JAMES M. PAYNE,
*Speaker Council.*

Concurred: JAMES BROWN,
*Pres't Nat. Com. pro tem.*

Approved: JNO. ROSS.

---

AN ACT to amend an Act, in relation to the salary of the Clerk of the Supreme Court, &c.

*Be it enacted by the National Council.* That an Act,

passed Dec. 8th, 1842, in relation to the salary of the Clerk of the Supreme Court, be, and the same is hereby amended, that the Clerks of the Circuit and District Courts, be paid a salary of twenty-five dollars a year, in addition to their *per diem* allowance for their services, during the session of Courts: and the Clerks of the District Courts, be allowed two dollars and fifty cents per day, for their services during Courts.

TAHLEQUAH, C. N., Nov. 27th, 1844,

JAMES M. PAYNE,
*Speaker Council.*

Concurred: MOSES DANIEL.
*Pres't Nat. Com.*

---

*Be it enacted by the National Council*, That there shall be printed, at the office of the Cherokee Advocate, at the expense of the Cherokee Nation, blank certificates for the use of Sheriffs and Clerks of the several districts, and all other officers of the Cherokee Nation, who issue certificates.

TAHLEQUH, C. N., *Nov.* 18*th*, 1844.

JAMES BROWN,
*Pres't Nat. Com. pro tem.*

Concurred: JAMES M. PAYNE,
*Speaker Council.*

Approved: JNO. ROSS.

---

*Be it enacted by the National Council*, That the Law, passed on the 5th December, 1842, entitled an "Act, to exempt property from public sale," be, and the same is hereby amended, so as to continue in full force and virtue, for the term of two years from the 5th day of December next.

TAHLEQUAH, C. N., 20*th November*, 1844.

MOSES DANIEL.
*Pres't Nat. Com.*

Concurred: RICH'D. DREW,
*Speaker Council pro tem.*

AN ACT Declarative of the rights of the Cherokee Nation, and authorising the appointment of a Delegation.

*Whereas*, The original and inalienable rights of the Cherokee people, "as a separate and distinct Nation," are not of recent origin, but have, in their essential elements, been enjoyed and exercised by our fathers, "from a period extending into antiquity, beyond the records and memory of man;"

*And*, *Whereas*, The present organization of the National Government was established by the rightful, and unconstrained assertion of the people's will, in the adoption of the Act of Union, between the Eastern and Western Cherokees;

*And*, *Whereas*, This Act of Union, and the Constitution based upon it, were confirmed and regulated in various forms, in the presence of the officers of the United States, and so reported to their Government;

*And*, *Whereas*, By the adoption of the said Act of Union, the distinction of "Old Settler" and "Emigrant," ceased and was done away; and "all right and title to public Cherokee land, on the east or west of the river Mississippi, with all other public interests, which may have vested in either branch of the Cherokee family, whether inherited from our fathers, or derived from any other source," was vested, "entire and unimpaired, in the Cherokee Nation," as constituted by that "Union;"

*And*, *Whereas*, The Cherokee Nation, thus constituted, has disbursed large sums of money, in payment of claims, originating under the laws of the Western Cherokees or "Old Settlers," without the slightest distinction being made between them and those who had been called Eastern Cherokees;

*And*, *Whereas*, In all departments of the Government, offices have been filled, by citizens formerly belonging to every class, justice has been administered and protection afforded to all; equally and without distinction;

*And*, *Whereas*, We deeply regret, that, in giving countenance to John Rogers and others, whose aim is, to form a conspiracy against the Government and integrity of the Nation; the Hon. Secretary of War should have evinced sentiments so greatly at variance with those of the President, and with the relations, actually subsisting, between the Cherokee Nation and the United States.—And especially, do we regret, that in opposition to the forcible and conclusive remonstrance of the Delegation, the Hon. Secretary should have appointed a commission to make enquiries in this country, under instructions inconsistent with our National rights, and dangerous to our liberties; and the direct tendency of which is to create factions, and to disturb the tranquility of the community;

*Be it therefore enacted by the National Council*, That a Delegation be appointed, to proceed immediately, to Washington, and by every means in their power, to maintain the rights of the Cherokee Nation, and to press upon the attention of the United States Government, the claims of the Cherokee people, both National and individual.

*And, be it further enacted*, That the Delegation be clothed with full powers to conclude a Treaty with the United States, and to do all other things, which may be necessary to bring all matters, in discussion, between the two parties, to a final close.

*And be it further enacted*, That in the event of any vacancy occurring in the Delegation, the Principal Chief is hereby authorized to fill the same by appointment.

TAHLEQUH, *Dec.* 18*th*, 1844.

MOSES DANIEL,
*Pres't Nat. Com.*

Concurred: ARCHIBALD CAMPBELL,
*Speaker Council pro tem.*

Approved: JNO. ROSS.

---

AN ACT for the benefit of James S. Price, Contractor.

*Be it enacted by the National Council*, That the sum of two thousand, seven hundred and seventy-five dollars and fifty cents, be, and the same is hereby appropriated, out of any moneys in the National Treasury, not otherwise appropriated, for the benefit and use of James S. Price, Contractor for building a Court House at Tahlequah, of the kind and description set forth in an Act, passed at the last session of the annual Council, authorizing the building of a "Court House."

*Be it further enacted*, That the Principal Chief be, and he is hereby authorized to draw a warrant on the National Treasurer, for the amount of the above appropriation, in the name of the said James S. Price, Contractor.

Tahlequh, C. N., *Oct. 22d*, 1844.

THOMAS FOREMAN,
*Pres't Nat. Com. pro tem.*

Concurred: JAMES M. PAYNE,
*Speaker Council.*

Approved: MOSES DANIEL,
*Acting Prin'l Chief.*

---

*Be it resolved by the National Council*, That the Principal Chief be requested to have the mortal remains of Ta-la-si-ni, late a member of the Council, from Canadian district, removed and decently interred, on a lot, to be hereafter used as a public burial ground.

*Resolved*, That the members of the National Council will attend, in a body, the burial of the deceased.

*Resolved*, That as a humble testimonial of the respect in which the memory of the dead is held, by the National Council, the Principal Chief is also requested to have placed at the head of his grave, a tomb-stone with the following inscription: Ta-la-si-ni, member of the National Council, from Canadian district, died at Tahlequah, October 26th, 1844.

Tahlequh, C. N., *Oct. 28th*, 1844.

THOMAS FOREMAN,
*Pres't Nat. Com. pro tem.*

Concurred: JAMES M. PAYNE,
*Speaker Council.*

*Be it enacted by the National Council*, That the sum of thirty dollars, be, and the same is hereby appropriated out of any money in the Treasury, not otherwise appropriated, for the benefit of Big James, or, O-ne-you-he-ter, for the year 1844.

TAHLEQUAH, C. N., *Dec.* 24*th*, 1844.

JAMES BROWN,
*Pres't Nat. Com. pro tem.*

Concurred: JAMES M. PAYNE,
*Speaker Council.*

DAN. M. GUNTER
*Clerk Nat. Com.*

J. MULKEY.
*Clerk Council.*

Approved JNO. ROSS.

---

AN ACT appropriating $300 00 to George Guess, for the year 1844.

*Be it enacted by the National Council*, That the sum of three hundred dollars be, and the same is hereby, appropriated out of any money in the Treasury, not otherwise appropriated, for the benefit of George Guess, or his wife Sarah, for the year 1844.

TAHLEQUAH, C. N., Dec. 24th, 1844.

JAMES BROWN,
*Pres't Nat. Com. pro tem.*

Concurred: JAMES M. PAYNE,
*Speaker Council.*

Approved: JNO. ROSS.

---

AN ACT relative to the Court House in Illinois district.

*Be it enacted by the National Council*, That the Court House for Illinois district be, and the same is hereby authorized to be located and built at Tahlonteesky, the old Council Ground, in Illinois district; and the law which fixed the site at another place, is hereby repealed.

TAHLEQUAH, C. N., *7th Jan.*, 1845.

ARCHIBALD CAMPBELL,
*Speaker Council pro tem.*

Concurred: MOSES DANIEL.
*Pres't Nat. Com.*

Approved: JNO. ROSS.

---

*Be it enacted by the National Council*, That all persons having houses, or other improvements on the public square, in the town of Tahlequah, be, and they are hereby required to remove them by the first of September next.

*And be it further enacted*, That should any person or persons, having improvements as above, fail or refuse to comply with the requirements of this Act, shall forfeit and pay a sum of fifty dollars; and all such fines, when collected shall be applied to National purposes.

TAHLEQUAH, C. N., Jan. 8th, 1845.

MOSES DANIEL,
*Pres't Nat. Com.*

Concurred: A. CAMPBELL,
*Speaker Council pro tem.*

Approved: JNO. ROSS.

---

*Whereas*, The depredations committed upon the property of certain citizens of this Nation, within a short time past, and many other circumstances render it notorious, that Thomas Starr and Ellis Starr, who with Bean Starr, murdered, robbed and burnt, with his store, in 1843, Mr. Vore, wife, and a traveller, citizens of the U. States; and Ellis West and Samuel McDaniel, who within a few weeks past, murdered, in an atrocious manner, two Cherkees, Tetaneskee and Chane Lacha, are clubbed with other bad men in this Nation, for the purpose of committing murder, and thefts, and arson upon the lives and property of our citizens; Therefore,

*Be it enacted by the National Council*, That the Principal Chief be, and he is hereby authorised to offer out of the National funds, a reward of one thousand dollars each, for the apprehension and delivery of Thomas Starr and Ellis Starr, to the proper authorities of this Nation; and five hundred dollars each, for Ellis West and Sam'l McDaniel. In case any of them should be killed in the attempt to apprehend them, the reward shall be given on proof of that fact.

TAHLEQUH, C, N., *Jan. 9th*, 1845.

MOSES DANIEL,
*Pres't Nat. Com.*

Concurred: A. CAMPBELL,
*Speaker Council pro tem.*

Approved: JNO. ROSS.

---

A Resolution repealing the resolution appointing the day for adjournment.

*Be it enacted by the National Council*, That the Resolution passed on the 7th ult., appointing to-day for the adjournment of the National Council, be, and the same is hereby repealed.

TAHLEQUAH, C. N., *Jan. 11th*, 1845.

JAMES BROWN,
*Pres't Nat. Com. pro tem.*

Concurred: ARCH'D CAMPBELL,
*Speaker Council.*

---

AN ACT to alter the line between Saline and Delaware districts.

*Be it enacted by the National Council*, That after the

passage of this Act, the line between Delaware and Saline districts shall be as follows: Commencing at a point on Spring Creek, where Going Snake and Tahlequah districts corner, and up the left hand fork of Spring Creek, by Switchler Lowrey's, and across to Oo-le stuhees' place, leaving him in Saline district; thence along the path to Oo-le-tah-tees' old place, leaving the said place in Saline; thence along a path on the ridge to Chee-li-o's place, leaving that place in Saline; and thence to a ford, a short distance above Ned Christies, on Spavinaw; and thence straight to the mouth of a small creek above Ned Persimon's, on Grand River; and thence across to Oo-law-nah-tee-skee's place on Cabbin Creek, leaving the said place in Saline; and up said creek to the Osage boundary line; and the Act passed 18th Dec. 1844, altering the line between Delaware and Saline districts be, and the same is hereby repealed.

TAHLEQUH, C. N., 13*th Jan.*, 1845.

A. CAMPBELL,
*Speaker Council pro tem.*

Concurred: THOMAS FOREMAN,
*Pres't Nat. Com. pro tem.*

Approved: JNO. JOSS.

---

*Be it enacted by the National Council*, That there shall be appointed, at the opening of each annual session of the General Council, a fire maker for each branch of the Council, and for the Supreme Court, whose duty it shall be to keep fires, carry water, &c; who shall be entitled to a compensation of fifty cents per day each for their services.

TAHLEQUAH, C. N., 13*th January* 1845.

A. CAMPBELL,
*Speaker pro tem Council.*

Concurred: THOMAS FOREMAN,
*Pres't Nat. Com. pro tem.*

Approved: JNO. ROSS.

## AN ACT relative to holding Elections.

*Be it enacted by the National Council*, That the Act, passed 4th Nov. 1839, organizing the Nation into eight districts, and for holding elections, and the Act passed 22d Nov. 1842, shall remain in force until otherwise altered by law, with the following amendments:

*Be it further enacted*, That the district Judges be, and are hereby authorized to appoint the Superintendants and clerks for each precinct, who shall be qualified by the district Judge or clerk to conduct the elections agreable to law.

*Be it further enacted*, That if a vacancy should occur at the holding of the elections, it shall be lawful for the people to fill vacancies that may exist.

*Be it further enacted*, That the Superintendants and clerks shall be entitled to a compensation of one dollar per day while in service.

TAHLEQUAH, C. N., *Jan. 11th*, 1845.

JAMES BROWN,
*Pres't Nat. Com. pro tem.*

Concurred: A. CAMPBELL,
*Speaker Council pro tem.*

Approved: JNO. ROSS.

---

*Whereas, It has been made known*, That P. M. Butler, Esqr., U. S. Agent, is about to remove from the buildings and improvements, known as the "Dragoon Quarters," and now occupied by him as an Agency; Therefore,

*Be it enacted by the National Council*, That the land included in the survey, adjoining the Fort Gibson Military Reserve, recently made by P. M. Butler, Esqr., U. S. Agent, for the temporary use of his Agency, and all buildings and improvements made thereon, by the United States, be, and the same are hereby declared to be the property of the Cherokee Nation, and are reserved for public purposes; and all persons are prohibited from locating or making improvements within the limits of tha said survey, without having first obtained the consent of the National Council, under the penalty of forfeiting the same for the benefit of the Nation.

*Be it further enacted*, That the Principal Chief be, and he is hereby authorized to appoint an Agent, whose duty it shall be, upon their being evocuated, to take possession, in the name of the Nation, of the aforesaid buildings and improvements; and having publicly advertised the same, for thirty days, to lease them, (the buildings and improvements) to the highest bidder, for the term of two years. The lessee of such buildings and improvements shall give bond and good security for the payment of the amount of his lease, into the National Treasury, in two annual instalments.

TAHLEQUAH, C. N., *Jan. 13th*, 1845.

THOMAS FOREMAN,
*Pres't. Nat. Committee pro tem.*

Concurred: ARCHIBALD CAMPBELL,
*Speaker Council pro tem.*

Approved: JNO. ROSS.

---

*Be it enacted by the National Council*, That the Editor of the Cherokee Advocate be, and he is hereby authorized to have alterations made in the stairway and partitions, in the Printing office, and a brick chimney erected with four fire places.

TAHLEQUAH, C. N., *January 16th*, 1845.

MOSES DANIEL,
*Pres't Nat. Com.*

Concurred: A. CAMPBELL,
*Speaker Council pro tem.*

Approved: JNO. ROSS,

*Be it enacted by the National Council*, That the sum of two hundred and eighty dollars be, and the same is hereby allowed to Daniel R. Coodey and company, for the apprehension of Bean Starr and the recovery of stolen horses in the fall of 1844.

TAHLEQUAH, C. N., *Jan. 8th*, 1845.

MOSES DANIEL.
*Pres't Nat. Com.*

Concurred: ARCHIBALD CAMPBELL,
*Speaker Council pro tem.*

Approved: JNO. ROSS.

---

AN ACT authorizing the quarterly payment of the Translator and the Printers in the office of the Cherokee Advocate.

*Be it enacted by the National Council*, That the Principal Chief be, and he is hereby authorized, upon the certificate of the Editor, to issue warrants on the National Treasury, for the quarterly payment of the salaries of the Translator and Printers, employed agreeable to law, in the office of the Cherokee Advocate.

TAHLEQUAH, C. N., *January 14th*, 1845.

THOMAS FOREMAN,
*Pres't Nat. Com. pro tem.*

Concurred: A. CAMPBELL,
*Speaker Council pro tem.*

Approved: JNO. ROSS.

---

AN ACT fixing the appropriation for the Delegation.

*Be it enacted by the National Council*, That the sum of four thousand one hundred and seventy-five dollars be, and the same is hereby appropriated out of any money in the National Treasury, not otherwise appropriated, to defray the expenses of the Delegation to Washington, and that the Principal Chief be, and he is hereby authorized to draw a warrant on the National Treasurer for the same, and that the said Delegation be required to keep a correct account of all necessary expenditures.

*And, be it further enacted*, That the pay of the members of the Delegation, for their services, shall be, and the same is hereby fixed at three dollars per day, to commence from the date of their leaving home.

TAHLEQUAH, C. N., *Jan.* 13*th*, 1845.

JOHN DREW,
*Pres't N. Committee pro tem.*

Concurred: A. CAMPBELL,
*Speaker Council pro tem.*

Approved: JNO. ROSS.

---

*Whereas*, The use of ardent spirits and other intoxicating liquors, is productive of the most demoralizing, and otherwise degrading and mischieveous effects;

*And*, *Whereas*, The laws of this Nation, prohibiting the introduction and sale of ardent spirits, are rendered inoperative, to a great extent, by the existence, along the line, within the States of Arkansas and Missouri, of distilleries, groceries and tippling shops; from which those deleterious articles are issued to the Indians;

*And*, *Whereas*, Murders and other crimes of the most atrocious and alarming character; the very rehearsal of which are revolting to humanity, are clearly traceable to the still-house and the grocery, as their source; Therefore,

*Resolved by the National Council*, That the Principal Chief be, and he is hereby requested, through such channel as he may deem proper, respectfully to ask, of the Governors of the states of Arkansas and Missouri, respectively, such co-operation, and the exertion of such influence, as in their wisdom they may deem proper, effectually to put a stop to the traffic, in ardent spirits, along the Indian lines of their respective States.

TAHLEQUAH, C. N., *Jan.* 10*th*, 1845.

JOHN DREW,
*Pres't N. Committee pro tem.*

Concurred: A. CAMPBELL,
*Speaker Council pro tem.*

Approved: JNO. ROSS.

---

*Whereas*, There are unsettled questions and points of interest which have long been pending between the Government of the United States and the Cherokee people;

*And*, *Whereas*, The rights and claims of the Cherokees, involved in those questions, have been fully and candidly recognized by the President of the U. States, in his letter of September 20th, 1841, and his views and feelings, in regard to the redress for which they ask ingenuously and unreservedly expressed, we cannot withdraw the confidence which we have reposed in the promises there conveyed to us; which assure us that "a deaf ear has not been turned to our petitions and that" much attention "has been given to the weighty and important sub- "jects, 'which' we had 'urged,' 'adding if all the sub- "jects presented by you on the part of your people "have not been fully considered and decided, you will be "able to satisfy them that it has been from no desire, on "our part, to slight or neglect the wishes or interests of a "Nation who have been for so many years, the steadfast "friends of the United States, and for whose rights and "interests this Government feels the strongest concern."

"I have looked over the several Treaties that have been made between the Cherokee Nation and the United States, and I find there promises of friendship on the one part, and of protection and guardian care on the other;

and I now promise you again; and through you, your whole people, that the protection and care so promised shall be given." Having declared his purpose to negotiate a new Treaty, the President proceeds, "you may assure your people that"—"not justice merely shall be done them; but that a liberal and generous course of policy shall be adopted towards them. Upon the ratification of the Treaty contemplated, which shall give full indemnity for all wrongs which they may have suffered; establish upon a permanent basis the political relations between them and the people of the United States—guarantee their lands in absolute fee simple, and prescribe specific rules in reference to subjects of the most interesting character to them and their remotest posterity, a new sun will have dawned upon them in whose brightness their permanent happiness and true glory may be read by the whole world."

***Resolved**, Therefore by the National Council*, In reliance on these just and elevated sentiments of the President, and in accordance with an Act of the National Council, passed Dec. 18th, 1844, that John Ross, P. Chief, Richard Taylor, John Looney, T. Walker, Moses Daniel, W. S. Coodey, Joseph Vann, Aaron Price and John Spears, be, and they are hereby appointed a Delegation fully to represent the Cherokee Nation before the Government of the United States.

***Resolved***, That the aforesaid John Ross, R. Taylor, J. Looney, T. Walker, Moses Daniel, W. S. Coodey, Joseph Vann, A. Price and Jno. Spears, be, and they are hereby invested with full powers to conclude a Treaty with the Government of the United States, and to do all other things which may be required for the final adjustment of all questions and matters of interest now pending between the parties, and bringing them to a final close.

***And be it further Resolved***, That the said John Ross, R. Taylor, J. Looney, T. Walker, Moses Daniel, W. S. Coodey, Joseph Vann, A. Price and J. Spears, be, and they are hereby authorized to apply to the Govern-

and they are hereby authorized to apply to the Government of the United States, or the proper officers thereof, and to receive all sums of money due on any account whatever, and receipt for the same, in the name and on behalf of the Cherokee Nation.

*Resolved*, That in the event of any vacancy occurring in the Delegation, the Principal Chief be, and he is hereby authorized to fill the same by appointment.

*January* 13*th*, 1845. THOMAS FOREMAN,
*Pres't Nat. Com. pro tem.*
JAMES M. PAYNE,
*Speaker Council.*

Approved: JNO. ROSS.

---

AN ACT making appropriations for the support of public Schools for the year 1845.

***Be it enacted by the National Council***, That the sum of seven thousand and two hundred dollars be, and the same is hereby appropriated, out of any money in the National Treasury, belonging to the School Fund, not otherwise appropriated, for the support of the public Schools, provided for by law, during the year 1845.

***Be it further enacted***, That the sum of three thousand six hundred dollars be, and the same is hereby appropriated, out of any money in the National Treasury, belonging to the Orphan Fund, not otherwise appropriated, for the board and clothing of the orphan children who may attend the several public Schools, the amount expended at each School, not to exceed the sum of two hundred dollars.

***Be it further enacted***, That the sum of four hundred dollars be, and the same is hereby appropriated, out of any money in the National Treasury, belonging to the School Fund, not otherwise appropriated, for the purchase of books, slates and stationary, for the use of the public Schools.

***Be it further enacted***, That the Principal Chief be, and he is hereby authorized to draw warrants on the National Treasury, for the amounts herein appropriated, in accordance with the provisions of the Act passed November 16th, 1843, entitled an "Act to amend an Act, relative to public Schools."

TAHLEQUAH, C. N., *Jan.* 14*th*, 1845.

THOMAS FOREMAN,
*Pres't Nat. Com. pro tem.*

Concurred: A. CAMPBELL,
*Speaker Council pro tem.*

Approved: JNO. ROSS.

---

AN ACT authorizing the making of a loan from the General and Orphan School Fund.

***Whereas,*** The public funds now in the National Treasury, are not sufficient to meet the debts outstanding against the Nation; Therefore,

***Be it enacted by the National Council,*** That there be a loan made from any moneys in the National Treasury, belonging to the General School Fund, to the amount of fifty thousand dollars, and out of the Orphan Fund six thousand dollars, to meet the debts outstanding against the Nation. The sum thus borrowed shall draw interest at the rate of two per cent. per annum, and be paid out of the public funds first paid into the National Treasury.

***Be it further enacted,*** That the Principal Chief be, and he is hereby authorized to draw warrants on the National Treasury, for the above named sum.

TAHLEQUAH, C. N., *Jan.* 17*th*, 1845.

MOSES DANIEL,
*Pres't Nat. Com.*

Concurred: A. CAMPBELL,
*Speaker Council pro tem.*

---

The Principal Chief having returned the above Bill, with his objections thereto, in writing, to the National Committee, the Committee and Council proceeded to vote on the Bill, when it was passed by a vote of two-thirds.

TAHLEQUAH, 18th Jan., 1845.

MOSES DANIEL,
*Pres't Nat. Com.*

A. CAMPBELL, *Speaker Council pro tem.*

# LAWS

OF

# THE CHEROKEE NATION.

PASSED AT THE ANNUAL SESSION

OF THE

NATIONAL COUNCIL,

1845.

---

*TAHLEQUAH:*

Printed at the Cherokee Advocate Office,

1846.

# LAWS
## OF
# *THE CHEROKEE NATION*,

## PASSED AT THE ANNUAL SESSION OF THE NATIONAL COUNCIL, 1845.

---

AN ACT to reduce the number of Executive Councillors to three.

*Be it enacted by the National Council*, That the number of Executive Councillors be and the same is hereby reduced to three from and after this date.

TAHLEQUAH, C. N., *Oct.* 9th 1845.

W. S. COODEY,
*Pres't Nat. Committee.*

A. CAMPBELL,
*Speaker of the Council.*

Approved: GEORGE LOWREY,
*Acting Principal Chief.*

---

AN ACT relative to trial, expenses &c. of assault and battery suits.

*Be it enacted by the National Council*, That from and after the passage of this act, prosecutions for assault and battery shall be tried only at the regular term of holding courts, and the jury empanelled at such terms for the trial of civil suits shall be competent to decide all such cases, and verdicts return as in civil cases provided for.

*Be it further enacted*, That all expenses attending the prosecution of such suits shall be borne and paid by the parties as in civil cases; and not by the nation.

*Be it further enacted*, That in all cases of personal abuse or injury sustained by violence, the party injured shall have redress by the recovery of damages at the discretion of the court (having jurisdiction) in such sums as may be determined.

TAHLEQUAH, C. N. Oct. 13th 1845.

W. S. COODEY,
*President Nat. Committee.*

Concurred: A. CAMPBELL,
*Speaker of the Council.*

Approved: GEORGE LOWREY.
*Acting Principal Chief.*

---

AN ACT to amend the "Act establishing the Judiciary."

*Be it enacted by the National Council*, That from and after the passage of this Act, it shall be the duty of the Sheriffs of the several Districts, when arrests are made of persons charged with criminal offences, to notify some one of the Judges having jurisdiction over such cases of such arrest, the nature of such charges, &c., as early as possible, and without any delay whatever, in order that a speedy public trial may be had, or such bail required as may be deemed necessary by the Judge, to be given by the Criminal to the Sheriff in bond and security for his or their appearance at such time and place as may be designated for trial

In case the accused shall fail to give the required bond and security within a reasonable time he, she, or they shall be brought to an immediate trial.

TAHLEQUAH, C N., Oct. 14th 1845.

W. S. COODEY,
*Pres't Nat. Committee.*

Concurred: A. CAMPBELL,
*Speaker of the Council.*

Approved: GEORGE LOWREY,
*Act'g Principal Chief.*

AN ACT repealing an act passed 23d, Oct. 1843.

*Be it anacted by the National Council,* That the act passed October 23d, 1843 to amend an act for the punishment of criminal offences, be and the same is hereby repealed.

TAHLEQUAH, C. N., Oct. 16th 1845.

A. CAMPBELL,
*Speaker of the Council.*

Concurred: W. S. COODEY,
*Pres't Nat. Committee.*

Approved: GEORGE LOWREY,
*Acting Principal Chief.*

---

AN ACT to amend the Judiciary act.

*Be it enacted by the National Council,* That the "Act establishing the judiciary," passed Sept. 23rd 1839, be, and the same is hereby so amended that in lieu of twenty-four jurors being summoned to try all criminal cases, there shall only be summoned twelve jurors, six of whom shall be competent to try all criminal cases, except such as may involve the penalty of death, and verdict return as provided for in said act of 1839. In all cases involving capital punishment there shall be twenty-four jurors summoned as before provided.

TAHLEQUAH, C. N., Oct. 20th 1845.

W. S. COODEY.
*President Nat. Committee.*

Concurred: A. CAMPBELL.
*Speaker of the Council.*

Approved: GEORGE LOWREY.
*Acting Principal Chief.*

---

AN ACT to allow criminals to testify in certain cases.

*Be it anacted by the National Council,* That it shall be lawful from and after the passage of this act, when two or more persons are charged with a criminal violation of law, and it is difficult to obtain testimony in favor of the prosecution, for one of the party so charged to be allowed to give testimony against the others and in behalf of the prosecution, and such person so testifying shall himself be exempted from trial in such particular case wherein he may thus be allowed to become a witness. Permission however to testify in such cases shall only be granted by the Court having jurisdiction over the matter and while in session and upon the application only of the Solicitors of the Several Districts for that purpose, or by the person conducting the prosecution.

TAHLEQUAH, C. N., Oct. 21st, 1845.

W. S. COODEY.
*Pres't Nat. Committee.*

Concurred: A. CAMPBELL.
*Speaker of the Council.*

Approved: GEORGE LOWREY.
*Acting Principal Chief.*

---

AN ACT to amend an "Act for the benefit of certain Blind persons."

*Be it enacted by the National Council*, That the first section of the Act passed Dec. 26, 1842, for "the benefit of certain blind persons" be, and the same is hereby amended, that in lieu of "thirty dollars annually" being allowed for the purchase of clothing, there shall be allowed twenty dollars annually for that purpose.

TAHLEQUAH, C. N., Oct. 22d, 1845.

W. S. COODEY,
*Pres't N'l Committee,*

Concurred: A. CAMPBELL,
*Speaker of the Council.*

Approved: GEORGE LOWREY,
*Act'g Principal Chief.*

---

AN ACT to amend "an act relating to public cooks."

*Be it enacted by the National Council*, That from and after the adjournment of the present session of the National Council, the number of public cooks provided for at each annual session of the National Council, be reduced from "six" to *two*. Provided, however, that the Principal Chief shall have authority at any call session or when it is expected that a large assemblage of the Cherokees shall be in attendance, to appoint an additional number, if he should deem it necessary.

TAHLEQUAH, C. N., Oct. 23rd 1845.

W. S. COODEY,
*President Nat. Committee.*

Concurred: A. CAMPBELL,
*Speaker of the Council.*

Approved: GEORGE LOWREY,
*Acting Pricipal Chief.*

---

AN ACT to amend an "Act respecting the issuing of Certificates."

*Be it enacted by the National Council*, That the Act passed Nov. 28th, 1843, be, and the same is hereby so amended, that the Sheriffs and Clerks of the Courts for the several Districts be, and they are hereby required, to make their Report of all Certificates issued by them, to the National Committee, during the first week of the Annual Sessions of the National Council.

TAHLEQUAH, C. N. Oct. 23d, 1845.

W. S. COODEY,
*Pres't N'l Committee.*

Concurred: A. CAMPBELL,
*Speaker of the Council.*

Approved: GEORGE LOWREY,
*Act'g Prin. Chief.*

---

AN ACT to amend "An act relative to estates ana Administrators."

SEC. 1. *Be it enacted by the National Council*, That the act passed 24th of Sept. 1839, relative to estates and administrators, be and the same is hereby amended so as to require Executors of Wills and Administrators on estates of deceased persons, to report annually to the District Judges at the regular term of the District courts held in July, the condition of, and all that may have been done by them in reference to the business, property, and effects of such estate as he, she, or they may have in charge.

Sec. 2. *Be it further enacted*, That Executors of Wills and administrators shall be entitled to a compensation of eight per cent, upon the amount of property and effects belonging to an estate, for their services, which shall be appraised by two or more persons, to be appointed by the District Judge under oath.

Sec. 3. *Be it further enacted*, That it shall be lawful for an administrator or other person having charge of an estate where there is money or property left, after settling the debts of the estate, and there are minor heirs, to apply a portion of such money or property to their education at the public schools in this nation, and any money or property so applied shall be charged to such heir as so much received of his or her portion of such estate.

Tahlequah, C. N., Oct. 29th, 1845.

W. S. COODEY,
*President Nat. Committee.*

Concurred: A. CAMPBELL,
*Speaker of the Council.*

Approved: GEORGE LOWREY,
*Acting Principal Chief.*

---

AN ACT relative to the appointment of National Solicitors.

Sec. 1. *Be it enacted by the National Council*, That the act passed 18th, October 1841, relative to Solicitors or Attorneys, and the act passed 30th October 1843, to ammend the same, be and they are hereby repealed.

Sec. 2. *Be it further enacted*, That there shall be elected by a joint vote of the National Council a Solicitor for each Judicial Circuit, whose duty shall be to prosecute in behalf of the Cherokee Nation all persons charged with criminal offences and who may be arraigned for trial before any of the Courts in their respective Circuits.

SEC. 3. *Be it further enacted*, That the Solicitors shall be elected for the term of two years, and commissioned by the Principal Chief, and shall be entitled to a compenstion for their services of three hundred dollars per annum out of the National Treasury, and before entering on the duties of their office shall be required to take the following oath viz:—"I do solemnly swear that I will as Solicitor for and in behalf of the Cherokee Nation prosecute all persons who may be arraigned for trial before any of the Courts in the Judicial Circuit assigned me, charged with criminal violation of the laws of this Nation, to the best of my skill and ability; and that I will not receive any fee, or remuneration from any criminal either directly or indirectly, but bear true faith to the Nation in all criminal prosecutions."

*Provided further*, That each Solicitor may if he shall deem it necessary and proper for the interest of the Nation, appoint a deputy at his own expense to act in his stead, and who shall be required also to take the above oath.

TAHLEQUAH, C. N., Nov. 3rd 1845.

W. S. COODEY,
*Pres't Nat. Committee.*

Concurred: A. CAMPBELL,
*Speaker of the Council.*

Approved: GEORGE LOWREY,
*Acting Principal Chief.*

---

RESOLUTIONS authorizing the Chief to appoint a Guard of six men, to guard the Public papers, Documents, &c.

*Resolved by the National Council*, That the Acting Principal Chief be, and he is hereby authorized to appoint a guard of six persons to be stationed at the residence of the Principal Chief, for the preservation and protection of the Books, papers, documents, &c., belonging to the Nation:

*Resolved further*, That each of the guard be allowed a compensation out of the National Treasury of Ten dollars per month, except the one who may be designated by the Chief to the command of the guard, who shall be allowed fifteen dollars per month:

*Provided, further*, That the Chief discontinue the services of this guard when he shall deem it proper or expedient. Compensation shall also be allowed for boarding the guard.

TAHLEQUAH, C. N., Nov. 5th, 1845.

W. S. COODEY,
*Pres't N'l Committee.*

Concurred: A. CAMPBELL,
*Speaker of the Council.*

Approved: GEORGE LOWREY,
*Act'g Prin. Chief.*

---

*Be it enacted by the National Council*, That William P. Ross, Editor of the Cherokee Advocate, be and he is hereby authorised to have a Brick house erected under his superintendency in the town of Tahlequah, Cherokee Nation, of suitable dimensions for a printing office to be completed before the next annual Council, the cost of which shall not exceed eight hundred dollars. And the act passed January 16th, 1845, authorising the Editor to make any alteration he might deem necessary to the stairway and to have a chimney put to the present printing office, is hereby repealed.

TAHLEQUAH, Nov. 7th, 1845.

A. CAMPBELL.
*Speaker of the Council.*

Concurred: W. S. COODEY,
*President Nat. Committee.*

Approved: GEORGE LOWREY.

---

AN ACT to amend the "Act for building Court-houses."

*Be it enacted by the National Council*, That the Act passed Nov. 30th, 1842, entitled "An Act for building court-houses" be, and the same is hereby amended, by striking out the word "Sheriffs" wherever it occurs in said Act.

TAHLEQUAH, C. N., Nov. 7th, 1845.

W. S. COODEY,
*Pres't Nat. Committee.*

Concurred: A CAMPBELL,
*Speaker of the Council.*

Approved: GEORGE LOWREY,
*Act'g Prin. Chief.*

---

*Be it enacted by the Natianal Council*, That a company of Lighthorse-men be organized consisting of twenty-six persons, for the purpose of searching after and bringing to punishment, all persons charged with murder, and house-burning and who are now at large and endangering the peace and lives of the citizens of this Nation.

*Be it further enacted*, That the Principal chief is hereby authorized to appoint and commission a captain and lieutenant who shall immediately select and organize a company of twenty-four men besides themselves and command them for the purposes set forth above, and are required to use all exertion and vigilance in ferretting out and bringing all such violators of law and personal security to condign punishment; and in case of refusal to submit or resistance on the part of such offenders, it shall be justifiable to kill them, or any person aiding them in resisting the enforcement of the laws of this Nation.

Be *it further enacted*, That the captain shall receive a compensation for his services at the rates of Twenty dollars per month—the lieutenant fifteen dollars, and each private ten dollars per month—and a reasonable allowance shall also be maue for all necessary expenses while in service, such as horse-shoeing, provisions, forage, ferriages, ammunition &c., and which shall be reported to the Executive, certified to by the officers of the company.

*Provided further,* That the Executive may dispense with the services of this light horse company when in his judgment the quiet of the country and safety of our citizens may justify.

TAHLEQUAH, C. N., Nov. 8th, 1844.

A CAMPBELL,
*Speaker Natr Council.*

The National Committee concur in the above act with this amendment that the lieutenant shall receive eighteen dollars and each private fifteen dollars per month.

W. S. COODEY.
*President Nat. Committee.*

Concurred: JOHN SHEPHERD,
*Speaker of the Council pro tem.*

Approved: GEORGE LOWREY.

---

AN ACT providing for the translation of the laws and constitution into the Cherokee language.

SEC. 1. *Be it enacted by the National Council,* That the Act passed 5th Oct. 1839 and the amendment to same of Dec. 14th, 1842, providing for the translation "of the laws of the Nation into the Cherokee language," be and they are hereby repealed.

SEC. 2. Be *it further enacted,* That the National Committee select and agree with some suitable person or persons to translate the "Act of Union," the Constitution of the Nation, and all laws which may be in force at the adjournment of the present session of the National Council, also the laws of the Western Cherokees as they existed at the time of the "Union" of the two branches of the Cherokee people, and to have the same published in one book as soon as practicable.

*Provided further.* That the laws of the Western Cherokees as in existence as above stated, be published under direction of the National Committee in the English language.

Sec. 3. *Be it further enacted*, That the National Committee allow such compensation for the services contemplated by this Act as may be deemed reasonable and proper.

Sec. 4. Be *it further enacted*, That in case any vacancy should occur in selection or appointment of persons under this Act, the Principal Chief be and is hereby authorized to fill such vacancy.

Tahlequah, C. N., Nov. 10th 1845.

W. S. COODEY,
*Pres't Nat. Committee.*

Concurred: A. CAMPBELL,
*Speaker of the Council.*

Approved: GEORGE LOWREY,
*Acting Principal Chief.*

---

AN ACT to repeal an Act appointing Solicitors.

*Be it enacted by the Nat. Council*, That the Act passed 3d, day of Nov., 1845, relative to the appointment of Solicitors, and the Act passed the 18th of October, 1841, relative to the appointment of Solicitors or Attorneys, as also the Act passed to amend the same, dated 30th Oct., 1843, be and the same are hereby repealed.

Tahlequah, C. N., Nov. 15th, 1845.

A. FOREMAN,
*Pres't Nat. Committee, pro tem.*

Concurred: A CAMPBELL,
*Speaker of the Council.*

Approved: GEORGE LOWREY,
*Act'g Prin. Chief.*

---

AN ACT authorizing the Chief to appoint a Committee of four persons for objects therein named.

*Be it enacted by the National Council*, That the Principal Chief be and he is hereby authorized to appoint a Committee of four persons, to repair forthwith to that portion of the Cherokee Nation now in a disturbed con dition, with such instructions, by the Chief, as shall enable said Committee to promote peace and other duties that the Chief may deem prudent to assign.

TAHLEQUAH, C. N., Nov. 17th, 1845.

A. FOREMAN,
*Pres't Nat. Committee, pro tem.*

Concured: A. CAMPBELL,
*Speaker of the Council.*

Approved: GEORGE LOWREY.
*Acting Principal Chief.*

---

AN ACT appointing the Editor of the Cherokee Advocate Mail carrier, and his compensation.

*Be it enacted by the* Nat. *Council,* That from and after the passage of this Act, the Editor of the Cherokee Advocate be allowed a compensation of Ten dollars per year for carrying the mail from Tahlequah, transmitting Newspapers, &c., to the Post office at Park Hill and back.

TAHLEQUAH, C. N., Nov. 17th, 1845.

A. FOREMAN,
Pres't *Nat. Committee, pro tem.*

Concurred: A. CAMPBELL,
*Speaker of the* Council

Approved: GEORGE LOWREY,
*Act'g* Prin. *Chief.*

---

AN ACT to punish attempts on rape.

*Be it enacted by the National Council,* That the Act passed September 19th 1839 for "the punishment of criminal offences," be and the same is hereby amended, so, that in case any Negro shall be convicted before the Courts of this Nation of attempting by violence to commit a rape, he shall be punished with one hundred lashes.

TAHLEQUAH, C. N., Oct. 17th 1845.

W. S. COODEY,
*Pres't Nat. Committee.*

Concurred: A. CAMPBELL,
*Speaker of the Council.*

Approved: GEORGE LOWREY,
*Acting Principal Chief.*

*Be it enacted by the National Council,* That the Superintendant of schools be and he is hereby authorized to locate and establish a public school at "Muddy Spring" in Flint district, in addition to the number already in operation—and one other school also in Going Snake district at, or near the residence of I. A. Few.

TAHLEQUAH, C. N., Nov. 18th, 1745.

W. S. COODEY,
*President Nat. Committee.*
A. CAMPBELL.
*Speaker of the Council.*

Approved: GEORGE LOWREY.

---

*Be it enacted by the National Council,* That the Superintendent of schools be and the same is hereby authorized to locate and establish a public school at a point, or spring, between Moses Daniel's and R. B. Daniel's in Delaware District, in addition to the number already established.

TAHLEQUAH, C. N., Nov. 18th 1845.

A. FOREMAN,
*President Nat. Committee pro tem.*
A. CAMPBELL,
*Speaker of the Council.*

Approved: GEORGE LOWREY.

---

*Resolved by the National Council,* That the resolution passed on the 15th inst., fixing the 22d inst. for the journment of the National Council, be and the same is hereby repealed.

TAHLEQUAH, C. N., Nov. 21st, 1845.

A. FOREMAN.
*President Nat. Committee pro tem.*

Concurred: A. CAMPBELL.
*Speaker of the Council.*

---

*Be it enacted by the National Council,* That the Superintendent of schools be and the same is hereby authorized to locate and establish a public school, at, or near Tahlequah in lieu of one located at Fourteen mile creek, which is hereby discontinued.

TAHLEQUAH, C. N. Nov. 26th, 1845.

A. FOREMAN,
*President Nat. Committe pro tem.*

Concurred: A. CAMPBELL.
*Speaker Nat Council.*

Approved: GEORGE LOWREY.

---

*Be it enacted by the National Council,* That all certificates purporting to be for services, &c., against the nation and issued by any of the officers under the act of the 28th November, 1843, and which shall not upon examination be found to correspond with the certified returns of such officers, shall not be considered valid or binding on the Nation.

This act to take effect on the adjournment of the present session of the National Council.

TAHLEQUAH, C. N., Dec. 1st 1845.

A. FOREMAN,
*President Nat. Committee.*

Concurred A. CAMPBELL.
*Speker of the Council.*

Ayroved: GEORGE LOWREY.
*Acting Principal Chief.*

---

*Be it enactad by the National Council,* That there be forthwith organized an additional Light Horse company to consist of twelve men, a captain and lieutenant to be appointed and commissioned by the Principal chief, who shall immediately select and organize a company of ten men besides themselves whose duties, duration, compensation, and allowance shall be the same as those provided for in the act passed 8th November 1845.

TAHLEQUAH, Dec. 1st, 1845.

A. CAMPBELL.
*Speaker of the Council.*

A. FOREMAN,
*President Nat. Committee pro tem.*

Approved: GEORGE LOWREY.

AN ACT providing for the Translation of the Laws of 1845.

*Be it enacted by the National Council,* That the persons selected by the National Council be, and they are hereby requested and instructed to translate the laws enacted at the present session of the National Council, as soon as practicable; and the Prindipal Chief cause the same to be published, (say 500 copies) and distributed through the Nation: and that the same be printed also, in the English language, for circulation.

TAHLEQUAH, C. N., 2d Dec. 1845.

W. S. COODEY,
*Pres't Nat. Committee.*

Concurred: A CAMPBELL,
*Speaker of the Council.*

Approved: GEORGE LOWREY,
*Act'g Prin. Chief.*

---

*Be it enacted by the National Council,* That the Acting Principal Chief be, and he is hereby requested to remain at the residence of the Principal Chief, at Park Hill, during the excitement in the country, for the purpose of giving correct information of the affairs in the Nation: and that a reasonable allowance shall be made for his board, while he remains at Park Hill.

TAHLEQUAH, C N., Dec. 3rd, 1845.

Concurred: A. CAMPBELL,
*Speaker of the Council.*

W. S COODEY,
*Pres't Nat Committee.*

Approved: GEORGE LOWREY,
*Act'g Principal Chief.*

---

AN ACT apppropriating Fifty Dollars to purchase Books for the use of the Public Schools.

*Be it enacted by the National Council,* That the sum of fifty dollars be, and the same is hereby appropriated, out of the "General School Fund," for the purchase of books for the use of the Public Schools of the Nation: and that the same be placed, by the Chief, in the hands of the Superintendant for that purpose.

Tahlequah, C. N., Dec. 4th, 1845.

W. S. COODEY,
*Pres't N'l Committee.*

Concured: A. CAMPBELL,
*Speaker of the Council.*

Approved: GEORGE LOWREY,
*Act'g Prin. Chief.*

---

*Be it enacted by the National Council*, That the "Act relative to public schools," be, and the same is hereby so amended, that from and after the 31st day of January next, the *arphans* placed in the public schools shall be boarded and clothed at the rate of thirty dollars, each, for the scholastic year; and the number of such scholars in the different schools shall not exceed one hundred and twenty, and be regulated by the Superintendent.—All such orphans so received into the schools shall be destitute of parents, and under the age of eighteen years.

*Be it further enacted*, That the third section of the Act passed 23rd December, 1843, amendatory of the "Act relative to public schools," be and the same is hereby repealed.

Tahlequah, C. N. Dec. 4th, 1845.

W. S. COODEY,
*President Nat. Committee.*

Concurred: A. CAMPBELL,
*Speaker of the Council.*

Approved: GEORGE LOWREY.
*Acting Principal Chief.*

DECLARATION of the National Council of the vacancy of the Sherriffalty of Flint District.

Whereas, the Sheriff of Flint District, William Griffin, has left the Cherokee Nation, and is now a "Refugee" in Washington county, Ark's, and having fled the country in violation of his duties as an officer, therefore,

The *National Council*, in view of these facts, do hereby declare the office of Sheriff for Flint Distiict to be vacant, and that the same be filled by Executive appointment as provided for in such cases by the Constitution.

Tahlequah, C. N., Dec. 4th, 1845.

W. S. COODEY,
*Pres't Nat. Committee.*

Concurred: A. CAMPBELL,
*Speaker of the Council.*

Approved: GEORGE LOWREY,
*Acting Principal Chief.*

---

AN ACT authorizing the Editor of the Cherokee Advocate to remove the Printing Press into the Court-ho at Tahlequah.

*Be it enacted by the National Council*, That the Editor of the "Cherokee Advocate" be, and he is hereby authorized, to remove the Printing Press, Papers, &c., belonging to the establishment, into the Court-house at Tahlequah, upon the adjournment of the present Session of the National Council, and to occupy the same for printing, until the time fixed for the next Session of the Supreme Court.

Tahlequah, C. N., Dec. 4th, 1845.

W. S. COODEY.
*President Nat. Committee.*

Concurred: A. CAMPBELL.
*Speaker of the Council.*

Approved: GEORGE LOWREY.
*Acting Principal Chief.*